THE SMELLY BOOK

PictureLions
An Imprint of HarperCollinsPublishers

To Benji Big Boots
The smelliest dog in the world

First published in Great Britain by Jonathan Cape in 1987
First published in Picture Lions in 1990
This edition published in 1992
Picture Lions is an imprint of the Children's Division,
part of HarperCollins Publishers Limited,
77-85 Fulham Palace Road, Hammersmith,
London W6 8JB

Copyright © Babette Cole 1987

Printed in Great Britain

THE SMELLY BOOK

Babette Cole

Have you ever thought how many

things are really very smelly?

contain the most
revolting things.

Smelly cabbage,

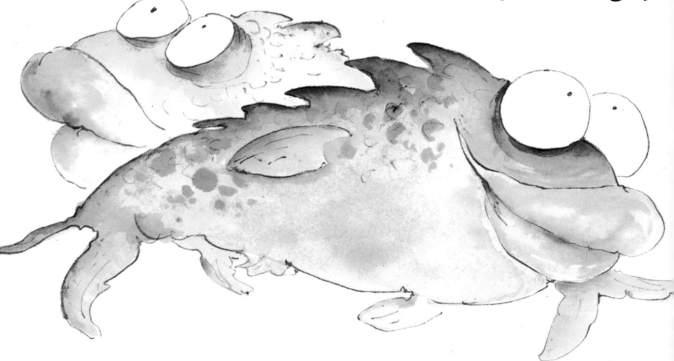

smelly fishes,

smelly cheese

for smelly dishes.

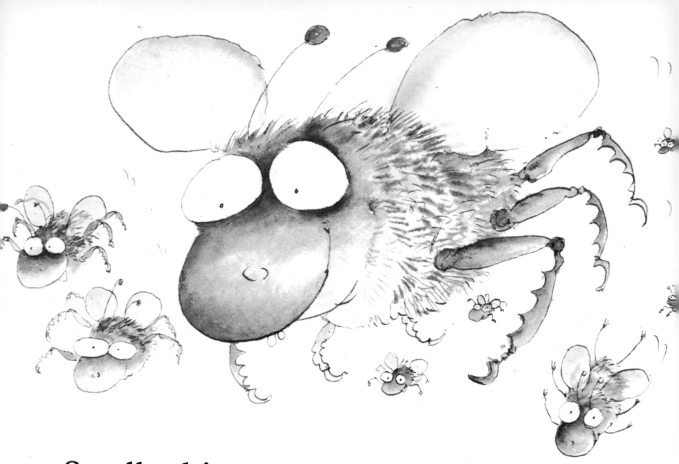

Smelly things attract the flies,
especially very old
pork pies.

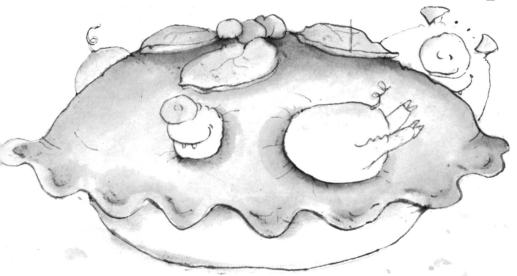

Camels have
a horrid pong,

warthogs can smell
very strong.

I think I would do a bunk

if I saw a smelly skunk!

Smelly pigs

and smelly mice

smelly ferrets are not nice!

Farmers are
a smelly bunch.
They can put you
off your lunch!

Stagnant puddles
smell so
grim...

hold your nose
when you
jump in!

Smelly socks that go quite stiff...

have the most disgusting whiff.

My dad's feet smell pretty bad,
sometimes it drives mum
quite mad!

Smelly bones make auntie swoon,

but smelling salts revive her soon!

Our dog likes to roll around

in smelly things left
on the ground

But if I rolled around a drain

I'd never see my friends again!

Smelly babies
wail and bawl.

Smelly tramps don't wash
at all.

Smelly kids play smelly tricks

because some grown ups are such twits!

Teacher said, "I smell a rat.
Who put this thing inside my hat?

...and who threw that rotten egg
at the science master's head?

Whoever did it was quite wrong

to blast the class
with that stink bomb!"

He kept us in 'til after tea.

But never found out...

It was me!